GRACIE'S
❧ BIRDS ❧

Other Books By
Fred Burstein:

Rebecca's Nap
Anna's Rain
Whispering in the Park
The Dancer
If It Snowed Forever
The Way to Cattail Pond
Animal Dreams

Gracie's Birds

By **Fred Burstein**

Illustrations by: **Rebecca Burstein**

IRIE BOOKS

Gracie's Birds is published by
Irie Books
Santa Fe, New Mexico
www.iriebooks.com

Graphic Design:
NRK Designs - Nancy Koucky

ISBN 978-1-5154-4804-4

DEDICATION

For Fran

Contents

ROBIN

ROBIN

This is Gracie's favorite kind of day —

Snow is falling all over the trees and bushes

And plenty of snow is on the ground to roll around in.

Gracie opens her mouth towards the sky

And catches snow flakes on her tongue.

"Don't eat too many, Gracie. They will give you a belly ache."

Suddenly she stands still with a front leg lifted off the ground.

An opossum is walking toward the winterberry bush near us,

Probably to eat some of its tasty red berries.

Gracie tiptoes over to the opossum and smells his head.

The opossum looks up at Gracie and opens his mouth,

Which has long gooey drips hanging out of it! He hisses!

Gracie barks and the opossum falls over onto the snow.

It looks like he just died!

"Come here, girl. Leave the opossum alone.

It will get up and look for food after we go away."

We walk closer to the winterberry bush and Gracie stops again.

"What is it now, girl?" I ask.

"Not another opossum, I hope."

Gracie walks even closer and barks as hard as she can.

Suddenly snow starts flying off the winterberry bush as robins,

Who had been quietly eating the red winterberry fruit,

Flap their wings in fright and head for the nearby trees.

BLUE JAY

BLUE JAY

Gracie wants to play outside,

But it is so cold and windy!

We walk past the snow covered garden where the sunflowers grew last summer.

We walk over the frozen fish pond.

We walk through icy trees that shiver without their leaves.

Gracie stops and lies down. She is very happy.

My feet are getting cold. I say, "Let's keep moving Gracie!" She looks at me and flops her head onto the snow.

I say, "Come on, girl, let's get going!" She looks at me and licks snow off her foot.

I say, "I'm starting to freeze!" She pushes her nose into the snow and sniffs around for a mouse.

Or maybe she smells a hibernating bear. Or a frozen thousand year old Woolly Mammoth deep in the ground.

I stamp my feet. I can't feel them any more.

A blue jay lands at the bird feeder and swings his beak back and forth making sunflower seeds go flying into the air.

Gracie gets up and shakes her body from her head to her tail. The snow flies off of her and on to me.

I say, "Thanks, girl."

On our way back to the house, we see the blue jay grab a fat sunflower seed and fly away.

GREAT BLUE HERON

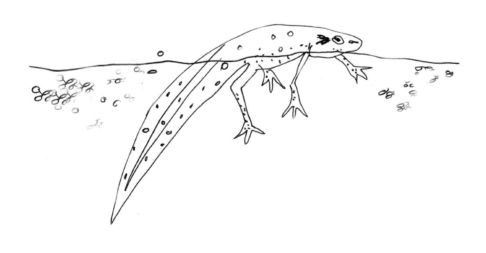

GREAT BLUE HERON

It's sunny and warm!

Daffodils are blooming but

There is still a pile of snow deep in the woods.

Gracie pulls me toward it.

We go past the melted pond

And see a newt floating in the water.

We go past the garden and I see the new sunflower plants popping out of the ground.

When we get to the woods, Gracie lies down on the left-over snow and takes a big bite.

I say, "Come on, Gracie. Let's keep walking!"

She looks at me for a second then bites the snow again.

A shadow sweeps along the ground. I look up.

"Gracie," I whisper. "Look into the sky. There's a Great Blue Heron! I think she is going to land in the pond!"

Gracie jumps up high and barks so loud and hard that the Heron flies back up into the sky,

Spreads out her enormous wings,

And floats away to her nest filled with light blue eggs.

❧ TUFTED TITMOUSE ❧

Tufted Titmouse

Even though it is still spring, the temperature is 95 degrees outside!

We had a long walk and Gracie can hardly lift her legs any more.

Finally she crumbles to the ground.

"I think we both need a break, girl. Let's go to the brook and cool off."

Gracie walks through the trees and lays down in the chilly water.

I take off my shoes and join her.

The water rushes around my legs and covers most of Gracie.

Only her head and her back stay dry.

We feel much better already.

Gracie barks. "What's the matter, girl?"

I look at her carefully. A little gray bird is standing on her back!

"That's a tufted titmouse! I think she wants some of that winter fur you're shedding."

The titmouse explores Gracie's coat with her beak.

She finds a thick tuft of winter fur just waiting to fall off.

Gracie looks up at me and barks again. She's not sure what to do.

But she doesn't move. The brook's water feels so good on her body.

"The titmouse must be building a nest near by.

Your old winter fur is just what she needs!

We have to brush it all off you anyway!"

Gracie tries to see the bird on her back and barks a third time.

The titmouse quickly flies into the forest

Carrying fluffy white Gracie hair to soften her nest.

OVENBIRD

Ovenbird

Gracie finds a tasty stick on the ground as we walk into the woods.

She is so happy. She lies down and begins to chew.

"We have to keep going, Gracie," I tell her. "The sky is clouding up and we have to head home soon."

Gracie looks at me with the stick in her mouth.

I can tell she isn't going to move.

I already feel some rain drops.

I lean over and put my hands under her belly and lift. "We have to go," I say.

Gracie scrambles to her feet, but she keeps a tight grip on her stick.

On the way home Gracie smells something in a pile of leaves.

She drops her stick and begins to bark as hard as she can.

Suddenly, a little speckled bird runs out of the pile.

She runs away from Gracie as fast as she can.

The bird is hurt. One of her wings is up and twisted.

I'm scared that Gracie will catch her.

Gracie barks again and rushes after the spotted bird.

I run after Gracie and yell, "No, girl!" But Gracie won't stop.

Gracie gets closer and closer to the hurt little bird!

One more step and Gracie will reach her.

But then the bird fixes her twisted wing and flies into the air.

I said, "She's an Ovenbird, Gracie! They build their nests on the ground.

She led you away from her babies!"

Gracie barked again and ran to find the Ovenbird.

But the Ovenbird was gone, safe and far away in the thick woods.

Pileated Woodpecker

Pileated Woodpecker

Gracie is lying on her back in front of the fan with her legs in the air. She won't get up. "Come on, girl. We have to go out for a walk," I say. "You can't lie here all day!"

She looks into my eyes. I'm sure she wants to say, "It's too hot outside! I want to stay in here!"

I hold out a treat to her and

She jumps to her feet, waits for her leash, and follows me out the door.

It's never too hot for a treat!

We walk past the garden where sunflowers are starting to bloom.

We pass the pond where the goldfish open their mouths and ask us for food.

We get to the woods where it is shady and cool —

And Gracie lies down on the soft green moss to finish her nap.

I sit down and lean back on a maple tree and almost fall asleep too.

Then we hear a loud banging and we jump to our feet, wide awake.

"What was that!" I ask, and Gracie begins to bark.

We bend our heads back as far as we can and look at the tree top.

"Gracie, it's a huge, black, white, and red Pileated Woodpecker!"

Gracie barks even louder.

The great bird grabs one more tasty bug from the tree bark,

And flies away into the bright summer sky.

Shoveler Duck

Yesterday, Gracie walked past our pond and went into the woods alone.

When she came home later, she was soaking wet.

She must have found a new place to swim by herself.

"Why don't you swim in our pond, Gracie?"

Today, just before she walks out of sight, I follow her.

I'm sure she can hear my feet crunching the leaves that have fallen,

But she keeps going.

Beyond the woods is a large meadow,

And in the meadow is a shallow pond.

I walk through the grasses and goldenrod and there's Gracie,

Walking in the water with two young Shoveler Ducks on her back!

More young Shoveler Ducks and their mother are swimming by Gracie's side, their wide shovel-shaped bills skimming the water for food.

When did Gracie become friends with ducks?

The young ones on her back are leaning over,

Scooping up bugs and plants like the rest of the family.

"Gracie, I didn't know you have secret buddies out here!"

Gracie almost barks, but she doesn't.

She doesn't want to scare her friends.

She walks out of the water, speckled with duckweed, and the two young ducks wobble on her back.

When she comes toward me, they fly off and join their family.

Gracie shakes the water and weeds off of her, and on to me,

And we walk back home to our family.

Ruby throated Hummingbird

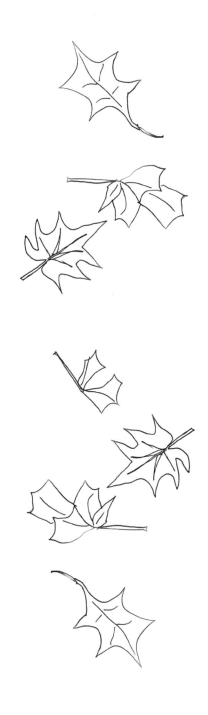

Ruby throated Hummingbird

Leaves are floating through the air.

Some are swirling around and around and some are swaying back and forth as they fall off the trees.

A swaying leaf lands on my shoe as Gracie and I walk past the garden.

I look at the tall sunflowers that are stuffed with seeds and bending over.

A swirling leaf lands on Gracie's nose, stays there for a second, and then falls into the cool water as we walk past the pond.

Gracie looks all around. She wants to ask, "What was that?"

"It's just a falling leaf, Gracie," I say.

"That's why we call this season 'fall!' "

Gracie slows down before we get to the woods so she can smell the orange and red jewel weed flowers.

Just then a tiny hummingbird comes to drink from the same jewel weed that Gracie is sniffing.

The hummingbird stands still in the air and sticks out her long tongue to drink some nectar from the flower.

Gracie takes a step and the bird's long tongue goes into Gracie's nose! She barks and jumps.

The hummingbird moves over, takes one sweet sip of nectar from the flower and flies south as fast as she can.

Glossary

ROBINS

I used to think that all robins flew south for the winter, but I found out that isn't exactly true. Lots of robins stay right where they are for the winter, even in cold areas where it snows and ponds freeze, like the place where Gracie lives. They can't eat worms and insects in freezing weather, but they do eat lots of berries and fruits. Hundreds, and even thousands, of robins roost in the same trees on winter nights. Robins that do migrate can travel 3,000 miles from mid-America to Alaska. And then they come back again in the spring. Both parents help build the nest on tree branches or in shrubs and they care for the eggs and the babies. The female usually lays four bright blue eggs that hatch in about 13 days. The female sits on the eggs, and doesn't leave them for more than a few minutes at a time. If you put all the worms that a robin can eat in a day in a straight line, the line would be about 14 feet long!

BLUE JAYS

Blue Jays are smart birds. Example: when Brown-headed Cowbirds lay their eggs in other birds' nests, a lot of those other birds hatch them. But if a Blue Jay sees a Cowbird egg in her nest she will eat it! Male and female Blue Jays look the same, but the males are a little bigger. When a female picks a mate, they stay together as long as they live. Together, they build the nest in tree branches (they really like oak trees), and while the female sits on the eggs, the male feeds her. When the eggs hatch in about 17 days, the male and female both feed the babies. They love caterpillars, by the way. After about three weeks, the babies and the parents leave the nest for good, but they all stay together for about two more months and generally they stay in the same area all year long.

GREAT BLUE HERONS

Great Blue Herons are really large. They have long necks and long thin legs and their wings spread out over six and a half feet when they fly. They look like pterodactyls in the air time-traveling from the age of dinosaurs. They live near wet places — rivers, lakes, and marshes and they hunt in the shallow water. They might stand still for a long time, or walk very slowly, looking for fish. When they see one, they spear it with their sharp beak and swallow it whole. They also eat frogs, crayfish, and snakes. They are the largest herons in North America and when it gets cold and water begins to freeze in the North they fly to South America for the winter. Both parents care for the baby birds in their large nest made of sticks. After about two months, the family departs and goes off on their own.

TUFTED TITMOUSE

The words "tit mouse" come from Old English, meaning "small bird." "Tufted" means they have a little wave, or tuft, of feathers on the tops of their heads. Tufted Titmice live in Eastern North America and the male and female stay together for life and live in the same area all year. They eat sunflower seeds, berries, caterpillars, moths, flies, snails, spiders, acorns, and beechnuts. If you are patient, they will come and eat from your hand. Typically, the female

Tufted Titmouse builds a home with the help of her mate in an old woodpecker nest. They also nest in boxes, and sometimes even in metal pipes. The nest is cup shaped. The mother bird uses damp leaves, moss, grasses, and bark strips to build it. She will line the nest with hair from raccoons, rabbits, dogs, like Gracie, and even people. Baby Tufted Titmice, or nestlings, are possible prey for snakes, raccoons, skunks, and squirrels. Adult titmice are also preyed upon by cats, hawks, and owls.

OVENBIRDS

They are called 'ovenbirds' because the nest the female builds looks just like an old fashioned outdoor bread oven. In spring and summer, when ovenbirds are in the eastern United States, they eat small bugs, worms, spiders and snails that they find in leaf litter in the woods. In the winter, when they are in Mexico and Central America, they eat seeds and vegetables. The females have a great trick to protect their eggs and chicks. When an animal gets near her nest, the female makes believe she has a broken wing and can't fly, and she hobbles away into the woods. She hopes the hunting animal will follow her and not find her nest. When the hunter gets too close, the mother ovenbird flaps her wings and flies away to safety.

PILEATED WOODPECKERS

Pileated Woodpeckers are the largest woodpeckers in North America. They have amazing bills that chip away at tree trunks when they are looking for food and making a nest. When they find a big bunch of carpenter ants or beetle larvae deep in a hole in an old tree, they can capture them with their long tongues. They chop out a new nest hole every year, usually in a dead tree and often in telephone poles. It takes them three to six weeks to dig the nest, which can be two feet deep. The male and the female both sit on the eggs, but at night only the male does. They do eat some fruits and nuts. The mother and father chew up the food for the babies before they feed it to them. They live in the same area all year long. Other birds, like owls and ducks, make their nests in the abandoned Pileated Woodpecker nests.

SHOVELER DUCK

The duck that Gracie meets is a Shoveler. The female builds a nest in the spring in a grassy area near shallow water. She forms a cup in the ground by twisting her body around and around and then builds a nest out of dried grass and lines it with her own soft down feathers. This duck is called Shoveler because its beak looks like a small shovel. It skims shallow water with its mouth open, then filters out the water with little bristles along the inside of its beak that keep in the small minnows, insects, shrimp and other crustaceans and some seeds and water plants. Northern Shoveler ducks go to southern North America and South America in the fall and winter.

RUBY THROATED HUMMINGBIRDS

Humming birds are the smallest birds in the world, and Ruby Throated Hummingbirds are some of the very smallest. They weigh only as much as one and a half pennies and they are as long as a dollar bill folded in half. They can flap their wings 50 to 200 times per second, and they can stay in one place in the air while sucking nectar from flowers. Hummingbirds can actually fly backwards. In winter they fly to South America; in summer they return north. Traveling back and forth each year they average about 5,000 miles in a year! There are some animals that might eat a Ruby Throated Hummingbird; for instance, cats, praying mantises, and frogs. The female builds a tiny nest on a tree or bush and usually hatches two eggs. She mothers her babies while the male bird fends off any predators.

GRACIE

And what about Gracie? Yes, she is a real dog. Her mom is a Maremma Sheep Dog and her dad is a Great Pyrenees Sheep Dog. Both breeds are very big and fluffy and have been protecting sheep as well as people for hundreds of years. When we go for walks, Gracie sniffs the scent of every animal that was there before us, and she looks around to find them. She would like to play with some of the animals, chase a few, and keep us safe from any predators.

FRED BURSTEIN has had many jobs over the years: child mower of lawns; teenage plower of snow; adult actor; and elder teacher of the young. But whatever the job, his real work was to write stories and have them become books. This is his eighth published book, and like the first seven, this one is about growing up with animals.

Fred Burstein and his wife Fran live in the foothills of the Catskill Mountains where their two daughters grew up playing in the woods, listening at night to owls and the brook below their bedrooms.

REBECCA BURSTEIN is Fred Burstein's daughter. This is the first book she has illustrated.

CPSIA information can be obtained
at www.ICGtesting.com
Printed in the USA
BVHW022315091121
621188BV00001B/10